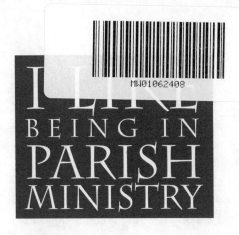

I LIKE
BEING IN
PARISH
MINISTRY

Eucharistic Minister

Nancy Gaudette

TWENTY-THIRD PUBLICATIONS
A Division of Bayard   MYSTIC, CT 06355

Acknowledgments

This book was inspired by my work in the Office for Worship, Archdiocese of Boston. It is an expansion of an unpublished work, *Service at the Table of God*, prepared by the Communion Rite Committee of the Boston Archdiocese Liturgical Commission and the Office for Worship. Used with permission. Some of the practical skills for eucharistic ministers were developed in conjunction with Mrs. Eileen Burke-Sullivan, a consultant and invaluable resource to the Boston Office for Worship. Some of the suggestions in the sections titled Preparation and Call to Serve were developed from the book *Liturgical Ministry: A Practical Guide to Spirituality*, by Donna M. Cole (San Jose, CA: Resource Publications, Inc.) Other editorial contribution to this book came from Rev. James A. Field.

Special thanks to Rev. James A. Field and Rev. Sean M. McCarthy, priests of the Archdiocese of Boston, for their encouragement in pursuing my Graduate Degree in Theology, for fostering my passion and love for the liturgy, and for their enduring friendship.

Twenty-Third Publications
A Division of Bayard
185 Willow Street
P.O. Box 180
Mystic, CT 06355
(860) 536-2611
(800) 321-0411
www.twentythirdpublications.com

ISBN:1-58595-151-X
Printed in the U.S.A.

Contents

Introduction

*The Eucharist constitutes the very life of the church, for the Lord
said, I am the bread of life. No one who comes to me shall ever
be hungry, no one who believes in me shall ever thirst.*

(This Holy and Living Sacrifice #1, *see Liturgy Documents*)

Over the years, I have had the opportunity to speak with
and train ministers of the Eucharist in various parishes throughout the Archdiocese of Boston. In so doing,
I have found that, often, the training provided at the parish level
for new ministers of communion consists of a brief session on
only one aspect of this important ministry, the practical skills.
The focus is usually on choreography: when to come forward to
serve, what to do when you are in the sanctuary, where to stand
when you serve communion, and what to do when the communion rite is finished. Although these skills are important, they are
not enough to fully be a eucharistic minister.

For ministry to be effective the formation provided must also
include an understanding of the theology and spirituality of worship. Otherwise, eucharistic ministry is reduced to just "giving

out" communion. And so in this book I hope to provide a solid sense of what the Eucharist means to Catholics. I truly believe that this is important for a minister's formation and must be included in a comprehensive training session.

Most articles and books written about eucharistic ministry contain the "how to" parts of the role but leave out the foundational theological and ritual pieces that help in understanding the ministry. Additionally, many Catholics are still unfamiliar with the documents that came out of the Second Vatican Council regarding liturgical renewal and the role of lay ministry. In fact, I would wager that most Catholics do not have a grasp of what we are actually doing when we celebrate liturgy on Sunday morning, or even why we do it. They are not aware that their role in the Mass is to participate fully, consciously, and actively. They have never been helped to delve into the deeper meaning of the communal celebration of the Eucharist and their responsibility within it.

When I have given workshops on the ministry of the Eucharist, I present the relevant documents and try to help participants understand not only their role as eucharistic ministers, but their role as part of the assembly. Many of the ministers in these workshops treat the material as if it were all new to them—and most of it is!

Based on this experience and a workshop series entitled "Service at the Table of God," I have provided in this book an explanation of the role of the eucharistic minister through a different but connected format. I have interwoven the "dos and don'ts" of eucharistic ministry into a detailed explanation of the Sunday celebration of the Eucharist. My sense is that this format will be easy to understand and will permit eucharistic ministers the opportunity to fully appreciate the Mass, and their role in it both as ministers and as members of the assembly.

This book also explores the significance of Sunday in the Christian tradition, the meaning of Sunday Eucharist through a focused look at the communion rite, the practical, theological, and ritual dimensions of eucharistic ministry, and basic parish visitation skills for eucharistic ministers who bring communion to the sick and homebound. These thoughts are intended to refresh you in your love of the Eucharist and in your appreciation of what the church asks of those who serve in the Sunday assembly.

CELEBRATING SUNDAY EUCHARIST

Since the very first days of the church, the day for the community celebration of the Eucharist has been Sunday. For the early Christians, whose neighbors consecrated this day to the sun, the day of worship was regarded in several different ways: as the Lord's Day; as the first day of the week, signifying a new beginning; or as the eighth day, signifying completion and fulfillment. The calendar in the United States puts Sunday as the first day of the week, and Christians still call this day the Lord's Day, the day when Christ defeated death and the Spirit blew upon the disciples (see *Catechism of the Catholic Church*, 2174).

In the *Constitution on the Sacred Liturgy* (CSL) which came out of Vatican II, we are made aware that our principal attention must be given to the liturgy, "the summit towards which the Church's action tends and at the same time the source from which comes all her strength" (*CSL*, 10). In his apostolic letter titled *Dies Domini*, Pope John Paul II writes:

> In the twentieth century, especially since the Council, there has been a great development in the way the Christian community celebrates the Sacraments, especially the Eucharist. It is necessary to continue in this direction, and to stress particularly the Sunday Eucharist and Sunday itself experienced as a special day of faith, the day of the Risen Lord and of the gift of the Spirit, the true weekly Easter. In learning to celebrate Sunday and its fullness, our relationships and our entire lives cannot help but become more profoundly human.

Sharing in the Eucharist is the heart of Sunday for all the baptized. Sunday is the day when Christians remember the salvation that was given to them in baptism and makes them new creations in Christ. Jesus gave us the gift of the Eucharist in memory of his life and death. This celebration makes us active members of his body.

How does baptism lead us to Eucharist? Baptism marks the moment in which all Christian life is born. In receiving the grace of baptism, we become a part of the body of Christ and are saved not only as individuals but also as members of the body. Having become members of the church, we no longer belong to ourselves but to Christ, who died and rose for us. We die to our old selves and become alive in Christ as the body of Christ.

Lumen Gentium (the *Dogmatic Constitution on the Church*) tells us that just as baptism is the source of responsibilities and duties, the baptized person also enjoys rights within the church; to receive the sacraments, to be nourished with the word of God, and "the right to receive in abundance the help of the spiritual goods of the Church" (37). Thus, the waters of baptism lead us to the table of the Eucharist and give each of us a place of honor at the table of the Lord, both on earth and in heaven.

Participation in Sunday Eucharist

The gathering of the whole community for Sunday Eucharist remains integral to our identity as Catholic Christians. The *Catechism of the Catholic Church* instructs us that, "the Sunday celebration of the Lord's Day and his Eucharist is at the heart of the Church's life" (2177). It is in the breaking of the bread that Christians experience and recognize the risen Lord. Through this communal celebration of the Eucharist we are sustained by one another's faith by sharing in the eucharistic meal of bread and wine. All are gathered together to pray. We form an assembly that performs the liturgical actions together.

"Assembly" is an ancient biblical word. It signifies that it is not the priest alone who prays, but all gathered who pray the liturgy together. The priest presides over the assembly and leads its prayer. He proclaims the message of salvation, joins the people to himself in offering the sacrifice to the Father through Christ in the Spirit, gives the assembly the bread of eternal life, and shares in it with them (*General Instruction of the Roman Missal* [hereafter *GIRM*], 60).

Paragraph 14 of the *Constitution on the Sacred Liturgy* states:

> Mother Church earnestly desires that all the faithful should be led to that full, conscious, and active participation in liturgical celebrations...to which the Christian people, "a chosen race, a royal priesthood, a holy nation, a redeemed people" (1 Pt 2:9, 4–5) have a right and obligation by reason of their baptism.

Thus, the principal concern of the liturgical reform that followed in the wake of Vatican II has been to promote the full and active participation in liturgy by all the assembly.

Our tradition describes four ways that Christ is present in the Eucharist: 1) in the assembly gathered, 2) in the person of the priest presiding over our worship, 3) in the word proclaimed, and 4) in the eucharistic meal of bread and wine shared. It is the presence of the Lord that fashions us into one body, the assembly of faith. The role of the assembly in Sunday worship is as the minister of the liturgical action. The assembly is not an audience. We are to take an active part in the dialogue and participate fully. We gather not just with the persons in our community but with the entire church throughout the world, as well as with those who have gone before us in death.

Know too that Christ is present in those assembled, in their praying and singing. As stated in Matthew's gospel "For where two or three are gathered in my name, I am there among them" (18:20). The assembly gathered together for worship makes the body of Christ visible in the worship space. We are a people called to offer God the prayers of the entire human family. We grow together in unity by sharing in Christ's body and blood. We give thanks for the mystery of salvation by offering his sacrifice. This is who we are: a people holy by their origin, but becoming ever more holy by conscious, active, and fruitful participation in the mystery of the Eucharist (*GIRM*, 5).

FOR YOUR REFLECTION

- How do you celebrate Sunday, the Lord's Day? Is it a day of quiet for you, one that is different from the rest of the week?

- Both baptism and Eucharist are sacraments of transformation. How do these two sacraments complement each other? How does the liturgy clarify the connection between these two sacraments?

- When you arrive for Mass on Sunday, do you believe that your primary role in the liturgy is to be an active participant? How do you express that belief?

Think about ways that you can better prepare yourself in your daily prayer to celebrate the Eucharist on Sunday. Bring your thoughts and prayers with you to the liturgy. Remember those whom you have promised to pray for, and include them in the prayers of intercession.

Remember that prayer is the gift of the Spirit. Paul writes:

Likewise the Spirit helps us in our weakness; for we do not know how to pray as we ought, but that very Spirit intercedes with sighs too deep for words. And God, who searches the heart, knows what is the mind of the Spirit, because the Spirit intercedes for the saints according to the will of God. We know that all things work together for good for those who love God, who are called according to his purpose....What then are we to say about these things? If God is for us, who is against us? (Romans 8:26–28, 31)

FOUNDATIONS OF EUCHARISTIC MINISTRY

The faithful should serve the people of God willingly when asked to perform some particular ministry in the celebration.
(GIRM, 62)

Pope John XXIII recognized that one of the issues facing the modern church was that many people were not living out the gospel in their daily lives. The message of Jesus was often difficult to perceive through the Mass, because the action involved mostly the clergy, who were somewhat hidden from view and spoke in unknown languages. Catholics did not fully participate in an active way in the liturgical celebrations, and the connection between liturgy and life was not made clear.

And so John XXIII called together an ecumenical council for the renewal of the church, that is, the Second Vatican Council. The fundamental goal of this Council was the unity of all

Christians. In addition to this, the Council sought to restore the assembly to its proper place as fully active participants within the liturgy.

Members of the early Christian church had varied responsibilities in assisting at Sunday liturgy. They greeted the members, read the Scripture, served at the altar, baked the eucharistic bread, and brought communion to those unable to participate in the liturgy. As the church grew, each of these roles became the responsibility of the clergy. Over time, the assembly was placed in a marginal role in which they were viewed as passive spectators instead of active participants.

While some Catholic laypeople had been deeply engaged in liturgical renewal since the 1920s, it is fair to say that most Catholics in the United States were not well prepared for the liturgical changes put forth by the Council. Yet in the thirty-odd years since the Council ended, lay ministry has had a tremendous impact on the life of the church.

The first appearance of laypeople as liturgical ministers was laymen who were permitted to read the first and second Scripture readings on Sunday. Later, laywomen were also invited to serve as lectors. Prior to the early 1970s, only a bishop, priest, or deacon could administer the Eucharist. In 1973, in a document entitled *Immensae Caritatis: Facilitating Sacramental Communion in Particular Circumstances*, Pope Paul VI gave permission to each bishop to authorize religious sisters and brothers and laity to administer communion. The ministry of communion was not considered an ordinary ministry for religious and laypeople, however, and so it was referred to as a "special" or "extraordinary" ministry, meaning outside the ordinary.

According to Vatican II, we all share in the priesthood of Christ through our baptism (see p. 10). Roger Cardinal Mahony of Los Angeles affirms this in a pastoral letter when he writes:

> Our duty is not just to be present; our duty is to be fully present. The songs are for singing, the Scriptures for listening, the silence for reflecting, the intercessions for pleading, the Eucharistic Prayer for immense thanksgiv-

ing, the Communion for every kind of hunger and thirst satisfied in partaking of the Body and Blood of Christ, and the dismissal for going out to love the world the way God does. (*Gather Faithfully Together*, 92)

The role of the assembly is to celebrate the liturgy together. It is not the priest alone who offers the Eucharist but all those gathered together who offer Eucharist "through him, with him, in him."

The Call to Serve as a Eucharistic Minister

Liturgical services involve the whole Body of the Church; they manifest it and have effects upon it; but they also concern the individual members of the Church in different ways, according to their different order, offices, and actual participation. (*CSL*, 26)

When people consider serving as eucharistic ministers, they may assume that their job will be simply to help the priest distribute communion and to speed up the celebration. They are not aware that the needs of the community are the basis for this ministry, that in their work as eucharistic ministers they are serving the entire community.

All liturgical ministers should be formed with an understanding of how their ministry affects all those gathered to celebrate liturgy. They need to be aware of their role in serving the assembly as a whole, and of how they help in building a unified assembly. The *Constitution on the Sacred Liturgy* affirms that laypersons who carry out specific responsibilities during the liturgy are considered to be ministers:

Servers, lectors, commentators, and members of the choir also exercise a genuine liturgical function. They ought to discharge their office, therefore, with the sincere devotion and decorum demanded by so exalted a ministry and rightly expected of them by God's people. (29)

In many parishes, the pastor appoints eucharistic ministers for a particular term. In other parishes, parishioners may offer their services to either the pastor or a member of the parish staff. Those who choose to serve in this ministry should be practicing Catholics who are known to be dedicated to growing in holiness. Eucharistic ministers set an example for the assembly at liturgy and thus they should also be examples of Christ in their community. Most importantly, ministers of communion should be especially observant of the Lord's command to love your neighbor, for when he gave his body as food to his disciples, he said to them: "This is my commandment, that you love one another as I have loved you" (John 15:12).

Eucharistic ministers are sometimes commissioned at Mass, in the presence of the community. Doing so articulates the significance and dignity which the church attributes to this ministry. One ritual that is often used is the Rite of Commissioning Special Ministers of Holy Communion. After the homily, the candidates for eucharistic ministry are presented to the assembly. Next, questions are asked of the candidates regarding their resolve to build up the church and to administer the Eucharist with care and reverence. The candidates then kneel and promise to accept this responsibility. Finally, the assembly is invited to pray for the candidates with the following words:

Merciful Father,
Creator and guide of your family,
Bless our brothers and sisters
May they faithfully give the bread of life to your people.
Strengthened by this sacrament,
May they come at last to the banquet of heaven.
We ask this through Christ our Lord. Amen.

(Book of Blessings, 1874)

FOR YOUR REFLECTION

- As a minister of the Eucharist, what qualities do you bring to this ministry?
- What concerns do you have with regard to your role as an extraordinary minister?
- How might you share your experiences with new ministers?

FOR YOUR PRAYER

Reflect on the following words:

> For just as the body is one and has many members, and all the members of the body, though many, are one body, so it is with Christ. For in the one Spirit we were all baptized into one body—Jews or Greeks, slaves or free—and we were all made to drink of one Spirit. Indeed, the body does not consist of one member but of many. (1 Corinthians 12:12–14)

HOW TO SERVE

As a eucharistic minister, you serve the community by sharing with them the mystery that makes us one body. Your scheduled time for service may not always be convenient, but it is always important. Your ministry is fundamental to the celebration and essential for those gathered.

If for any reason you cannot serve at a time for which you are scheduled, you should secure a replacement or notify the person in charge of the eucharistic ministers. Each parish should have a schedule for eucharistic ministers so that you know ahead of time when you are scheduled to serve. Mark your assigned days on the calendar. If you have any conflicts, notify the coordinator of scheduling as soon as possible. Or, if your parish hands out a master list with the names and phone numbers of eucharistic ministers, you can contact a replacement yourself.

Preparation to Serve

Preparation for liturgy begins when we rise on Sunday morning. On the day of your assignment, take some time for quiet prayer. If you know what the readings are for that day (parish bulletins often include the three Scripture readings), you may want to read one or all, taking time to reflect on the words. This preparation will help you make better connections between the homily and your own life, as well as put you in the proper mindset for ministry. As you pray, you may want to remember the community you are preparing to serve.

In addition to preparing yourself spiritually in prayer, it is also important to prepare your appearance. You should dress properly to reflect the importance and dignity of the ministry in which you serve. Your clothes should be what used to be referred to as "Sunday best." This does not mean expensive or fancy; but it does mean clothing that is neat, clean, and reasonably modest. Observe good habits of personal hygiene, including neatly trimmed and clean fingernails. Noisy jewelry, glittering nail polish, tee shirts with slogans, political buttons, and novelties such as musical ties should be left at home. The focus should be on the Eucharist, so avoid any attire that brings attention to you.

When you get to church, be prepared to participate in the liturgy with the worshiping community and not be preoccupied with the details of your service. And remember that your preparation for Sunday Eucharist must continue into day-to-day life with your family and friends during the week. This is not just about fulfilling a function on Sunday morning; it is not just a role where you give out communion or help the priest. It is a sharing in the very life of Christ as you are connected to the assembly of believers.

Your Assignment

On the day you are scheduled to serve, you should arrive in ample time, at least ten to fifteen minutes before the Mass is scheduled to start. This will allow you to not feel rushed and provide you the opportunity to center yourself in the presence of the Lord.

Parishes usually require that you check in with someone upon arrival to ensure that enough ministers are present and to receive your location assignment. Instruction for special changes may be given at that time, as well. (If you are not scheduled to serve on a particular Sunday, you may want to check in anyway to see if your service may be needed.)

Find out if everything is prepared for liturgy. Is there enough unconsecrated bread? Is there an appropriate amount of wine set out? The bread and wine we share at Mass should be consecrated at the same liturgy. This procedure may seem unrealistic but it is what is required of us:

> It is most desirable that the faithful receive the Lord's body from hosts consecrated at the same Mass and that…they share in the chalice. Then even through the signs communion will stand out more clearly as a sharing in the sacrifice actually being celebrated. (*GIRM*, 56)

Once all the tasks are complete, prepare yourself to enter into the eucharistic celebration as part of the worshiping community.

Hospitality

The practice of extending and receiving hospitality is deeply rooted in Scripture. Think of the story of Abraham and Sarah and the three guests. When Abraham saw the men approaching, he ran from the entrance of the tent to greet them. Bowing to the ground, he said,

> "My lord, if I find favor with you, do not pass by your servant. Let a little water be brought, and wash your feet, and rest yourselves under the tree. Let me bring a little bread, that you may refresh yourselves, and after that you may pass on—since you have come to your servant." So they said, "Do as you have said." (Genesis 18:3–5)

As ministers of communion, we are encouraged to warmly greet people before and after Mass, offering hospitality to the community. It is important to greet everyone who enters the doors of the church. Take time to greet both those you know and those you do not know. This gesture of welcome helps you to become more aware of the presence of Christ in yourself and in the people gathering for worship. In turn, your gesture of reverence for the members of the community helps the faithful to recognize Christ in one another. Through this sharing, we come to see we are part of the body that is the church, and therefore, open to transformation into the body of Christ at worship.

If you see someone come into church with a physical disability, ask them if they would like to come forward at communion to receive or if they would like the Eucharist brought to them. Do not assume that someone with a disability is unwilling or unable to join in the procession. I once knew a remarkable blind women who insisted that she not be left out of the communion procession, and each Sunday walked down the aisle with everyone else to receive communion.

FOR YOUR REFLECTION

- How do you greet guests in your home? Do you meet them at the door and welcome them with a smile? How might you carry this hospitality to Sunday Mass?

- Do you welcome the stranger at liturgy or do you spend time in conversation only with those you know? Reflect on a typical Sunday Eucharist in your parish and how you treat the people you serve.

- Think about times in your life when you have had an experience of someone sharing freely with you. How does this experience relate to your sharing of eucharistic bread and the cup of salvation?

FOR YOUR PRAYER

Reflect on the following words:

Rejoice in hope, be patient in suffering, persevere in prayer. Contribute to the needs of the saints; extend hospitality to strangers. Bless those who persecute you; bless and do not curse them. Rejoice with those who rejoice, weep with those who weep. Live in harmony with one another; do not be haughty, but associate with the lowly; do not claim to be wiser than you are. Do not repay anyone evil for evil, but take thought for what is noble in the sight of all. If it is possible, so far as it depends on you, live peaceably with all. (Romans 12:12–18)

THE LITURGY OF THE WORD

In the presence of God and of Christ Jesus, who is to judge the living and the dead, and in view of his appearing and his kingdom, I solemnly urge you: Proclaim the message, be persistent whether the time is favorable or unfavorable; convince, rebuke, and encourage, with the utmost patience in teaching. (2 Timothy 4:1–2)

The gathering rites begin the liturgy. Still, we may ask, when are we actually late for Mass? Prior to Vatican II, the answer to that question would have been that we must be in our pew prior to the proclamation of the gospel. Today, we would say that someone arriving even at the responsorial psalm is late!

As mentioned before, we begin preparing for liturgy when we rise in the morning, as we ready ourselves and perhaps our families. In our busyness we prepare to gather into one assembly.

My house on Sunday morning, like many, I'm sure, can be very chaotic. My daughters fuss over whose turn it is to use the bathroom and what they will wear, while my son plays with his trucks instead of getting ready. As we hurry out the door and drive to church, I try to encourage everyone to use the travel time as a transition from our "house church" to the "parish church." Throughout the week, as we have lived out our daily mission of loving and serving God, we have been preparing ourselves for the celebration of Sunday liturgy, for coming back together as the larger family of God to be spiritually nourished once again.

The purpose of the gathering rites is "that the faithful coming together take on the form of a community and prepare themselves to listen to God's word and celebrate the eucharist properly" (*GIRM*, 24). The document goes on to state that the purpose of the song is "to open the celebration, intensify the unity of the gathered people, lead their thoughts to the mystery of the season or feast, and accompany the procession of priest and ministers" (*GIRM*, 25). The opening song makes it possible for us to join in one voice as one united body.

Normally eucharistic ministers do not enter and exit the celebration in the liturgical procession. Exceptions to this may take place on special feasts or in communities that dismiss ministers from the assembly to bring communion to the sick. If parish practice includes you in the procession, be sure to carry hymnals with you and participate fully by singing as you process. Do not process with an attitude of self-importance regarding those you pass by in the pews; remember, you are all part of the same body gathered in worship.

When you arrive at the altar, reverence it with a profound, low bow. The altar "is by its very nature a table of sacrifice and at the same time a table of the paschal banquet" (*Dedication of a Church and an Altar*, chapter IV, 4). To reverence the altar is an act of greeting that evokes the holiness and sacredness of the table. Henri Nouwen referred to the table as one of the most intimate places in our lives. He said it is there that we give ourselves to one another as we invite our friends to become part of our lives.

Ministers should move with a sense of purpose, unhurried, to a place in the assembly for the completion of the gathering rites. In the opening prayer, the assembly is invited to pray together with the priest (*GIRM*, 32). This clearly means that it is not time for the priest to pray for us, but for us to be praying together. When the priest says "Let us pray," it is an invitation to all those gathered to join in the prayer. These rites serve to prepare us for the liturgy of the word and the liturgy of the Eucharist. They help us become a worshiping community in response to God's call.

Ordinarily ministers should sit in the assembly with their family or friends. I prefer to sit with my family because it offers a strong sign to both my family and the gathered assembly when they see me—and the other eucharistic ministers—come from within the assembly to serve. If you do not sit in the assembly, however, it is recommended you sit in close proximity to the altar area in order to move there easily during the sign of peace.

In every liturgy, ministers should demonstrate full, conscious, and active participation throughout the celebration. Recall again the words from the *Constitution on the Sacred Liturgy*:

> This full and active participation by all the people is the aim to be considered before all else. For it is the primary and indispensable source from which the faithful are to derive the true Christian spirit.

This includes singing the hymns (no matter how you think your voice sounds), answering responses, and participating in the posture of the assembly at each part of the celebration. Your participation is an example for the assembly.

Liturgy of the Word

Continue to participate in the liturgy of the word by listening attentively as the Scripture readings are proclaimed. If you have spent time preparing the readings during the week you will be able to enter into the word more fully.

In my family, each night before we begin dinner, we say a

prayer of thanks and blessing, and pray for the needs of those we love. We then take time to read the gospel of the day. On Saturday evening, we read the gospel for Sunday, then spend time talking about it and how it impacts our lives. This practice helps us all to enter more fully into the Sunday celebration of the liturgy of the word.

It is important to remember that in the ritual of the Mass we insert ourselves into the life, death, and resurrection of Jesus. Through this ritual, we grow to be part of the story, and we open ourselves to Jesus becoming part of our lives. We are transformed in our encounter with Christ as we connect liturgy to life. When the word is broken open in the homily, it helps us to remember we are disciples of Christ.

At the conclusion of the liturgy of the word, we continue our active participation in the preparation of the table and gifts. We collect money for the church and for the poor, and present our gifts of bread and wine to God. In these gifts we offer our very selves—our joys and our sorrows, the successes we have had during the week in our work or with our families, the struggles that we endure each and every day. All of this is brought forward and offered to God.

A woman I know once helped the parish bake bread for a First Communion celebration. She said that as she made the bread, she prayed for those who would receive it that they would grow in their understanding of Eucharist. She felt she was "praying them into the bread." When she actually saw the bread being brought forward in procession to the altar, she realized for the very first time that *she* was in the bread. It contained the work of her human hands and her prayers over the bread. This woman's life was joined with the assembly in that bread as it was brought forward and offered to God.

And so we move from the table of the word to the table of thanksgiving and communion. This is our ritual response to the word of God.

FOR YOUR REFLECTION

- Think about the importance of the proclamation of the word of God. How is God speaking to you through the person of the lector? How does the homily help you to break open the word?
- The Mass is divided into two ritual parts: the liturgy of the word and the liturgy of the Eucharist. What is the difference between how we are nourished at the table of the word, and how we are nourished at the table of the Eucharist?
- Think about the preparations you make for a dinner party at your home. Perhaps you set the table with candles, flowers, and the best china. In the sharing of that meal as family and friends, reflect on how those gathered at the table become one. How does this relate to the celebration of Eucharist?

FOR YOUR PRAYER

Reflect on the following words:

In the beginning was the Word, and the Word was with God, and the Word was God. He was in the beginning with God. All things came into being through him, and without him not one thing came into being. What has come into being in him was life, and the life was the light of all people....And the Word became flesh and lived among us, and we have seen his glory, the glory as of a father's only son, full of grace and truth. (John 1:1–4, 14)

THE
LITURGY
OF THE
EUCHARIST

The liturgy of the Eucharist begins after the presentation of the gifts, with the eucharistic prayer. The prayer starts by emphasizing our past experience of God and moves to the future. The presider speaks this great prayer as part of the assembly. It is our prayer. The eucharistic prayer is about the transformation of the gifts on the table of bread and wine, but it is also about the transformation of us.

When I offer workshops for eucharistic ministers, I often ask the ministers gathered to reflect on sentences from various eucharistic prayers, for example, "From age to age you gather a people to yourself," or "Make us worthy to stand in your presence and serve you." Ministers are astounded as they think of the words anew and try to explain the deeper meanings they feel in their hearts. Many participants have stated that they have heard the words spoken so many times by the priest that they have never really thought about their meaning or that they were praying it too. There is a profound sense that they are hearing the words for the first time.

As we celebrate in prayer and unite ourselves as one body in Christ at liturgy, we start to become who we are intended to be. We place our need for conversion on the eucharistic table along with Christ. We pray for the grace to accept suffering as Christ freely accepted the cross. We give our lives to God. God accepts our joys and our brokenness and makes them holy, giving them back as the body and blood of Christ.

Overview of the Communion Rite

The communion rite inspires and demands our reverence. Those who minister at the Lord's table share in a simple task, yet it is one that lives at the heart of who we are as Christian people. The communion rite perfectly clarifies the words of the memorial acclamation: "When we eat this bread and drink this cup, we proclaim your death, Lord Jesus, until you come in glory."

The rite begins with the Lord's Prayer and ends with the prayer after communion. The act of eating and drinking the Lord's body and blood together as one is the culmination of our Sunday worship. It is our hope of sharing in the banquet of the Lord's reign in heaven.

In Luke's gospel, we find the account of the disciples on the road to Emmaus (Luke 24:13–35). When the disciples encountered Jesus on the road, they did not recognize him and thought he was a stranger. They offered Jesus hospitality and a meal. Scripture continues: "When he was at the table with them, he took bread, blessed and broke it, and gave it to them. Then their eyes were opened, and they recognized him; and he vanished from their sight" (Luke 24:30–31). In this action, Jesus reversed the roles; instead of a guest in their home he became the host at the table. Likewise at liturgy, Jesus is the host of the meal and we are the disciples.

The Lord's Prayer

After the assembly sings the great Amen, the Lord's Prayer begins the communion rite. The assembly calls upon God as Father, using the prayer taught to us by Christ. In our preparation for communion, we offer this prayer for daily bread, prayed together for the kingdom of peace and unity as we learn how to forgive as we have been forgiven.

Please note that holding hands during the Lord's Prayer is not a ritual part of the Order for Mass. Some parishes who encourage this gesture feel that holding hands helps create a sense of unity within the body of Christ. Yet often, not all those gathered are inclined to hold hands, and so the posture becomes varied for the prayer. Thus, it is best to use the posture designated by the ritual especially since unity is fully created in communion.

The Sign of Peace

The rite of peace follows the Lord's Prayer. In Romans 16:16, Paul tells the Christian community to "greet one another with a holy kiss." This ritual action offers the special peace of Christ, and is not just a simple gesture of good wishes to those around us. (Although a friend of mine comments that this is the time to thank those around her for their patience and to apologize for the behavior of her five children!) The sign of peace is a reminder of Christ's parting gift to the church. We look ahead to the gift of everlasting life and wish this for all gathered. This action signifies that we are about to enter into communion with each other and with Christ.

During the sign of peace, ministers may exchange with those around them a warm embrace or a simple handshake accompanied by the greeting, "Peace be with you." This should be done before you move to the sanctuary. Take time to look at the person and recall that Christ is present in them. The peace of God is ours in the saving mystery of Christ. Thus, in exchanging a sign of the Lord's peace with one another we acknowledge our belief that Christ is present in the assembly.

After the sign of peace, the eucharistic ministers move directly to the altar area, bowing to the altar before entering the sanctuary. We do this because when the altar is dedicated, it is consecrated with the oil of chrism just as we are anointed with oil on the day of our baptism. The table becomes Christ just as we become Christ on the day we are baptized.

The Breaking of the Bread

All eucharistic ministers should be in the appropriate place at the altar before the presider begins the breaking of the bread and the pouring of the cups. There should be no movement in the sanctuary at this time. Everyone's attention should be focused on the table, on the action of the breaking of the bread. We believe that the bread is broken just as the body of Christ was broken for us on the cross. We believe that the wine is poured out just as the blood of Christ was poured out on the cross. Thus, we should stand reverently and attentively during this part of the rite.

This action is so important to our understanding of Christ's ministry and his assurance to be with us that the early church referred to the whole eucharistic celebration as "the breaking of the bread." Recall the story of the disciples on the road to Emmaus. Christ was revealed in the breaking of the bread. This action powerfully expresses our shared life together. Just as when a family gathers at the table for dinner, their lives become intimately connected during the sharing of the meal.

In the chapter on requisites for celebrating Mass, the *General Instruction of the Roman Missal* states that the action of the breaking of the bread "means that all are united in mutual love through the one bread, since this one bread is shared among many brethren" (283). All who share in this one bread become one body in Christ. We come to the table broken and we are restored as one in him. The bread of his body is broken and the blood of his sacrifice is poured out.

The nature of the sign demands that the material for the eucharistic celebration truly have the appearance of food:

> The bread must be made only from wheat and must have been baked recently. (*GIRM*, 282)

31

The wine for the eucharist must be from the fruit of the vine (see Luke 22:18), natural, and pure, that is not mixed with any foreign substance. (*GIRM*, 284)

In ancient times, the people brought the bread and wine from their homes. St. Augustine wrote that his mother would never let a day pass without bringing her offering of bread to the altar. Today, some parishes have a bread-baking ministry. This allows parishioners the opportunity to bake the bread with loving hands and pray for those who will receive it. A woman involved in the ministry of baking bread in my parish says that since she was unable to bake bread for Jesus' Last Supper, she is grateful that she can bake for the parish meal.

The bread used at Mass should be baked fresh for the celebration and prepared with only wheat flour and water. Nothing else can be added to sweeten or to change the taste or texture of the bread. (The *Sacristy Manual* published by Liturgy Training Publications contains an approved recipe for baking bread.)

When my mother died, I asked the bread-baking ministry in our parish to bake the bread for her funeral Mass. I knew that as they baked, they would pray for my family and friends that when we ate the bread we would know the joy and celebration of God's love. At the funeral, as I watched my children carry the gifts of bread and wine forward during the preparation rite, I knew that all of our lives were in the bread being offered, bread "which earth has given and human hands have made." Sharing this final earthly meal with my mother helped to sustain and nourish us in our grief.

During the breaking of the bread and the pouring of the wine, the Lamb of God is sung. Eucharistic ministers should participate in singing the responses to this prayer. The invocation and response may be repeated as often as necessary to accompany the breaking of the bread and the pouring of the wine in preparation for communion. The final verse concludes with the words, "grant us peace."

Once all the cups and plates are prepared, the presider raises a cup and plate and shows both to those gathered. The presider then formally invites all to communion. "This is the Lamb of God who takes away the sins of the world" (John 1:29), followed by "Happy are those who are called to his supper" (Revelation 19:9). The priest and the people respond together, "Lord, I am not worthy to receive you but only say the word and I shall be healed" (Matthew 8:8). At this point, communion is distributed to those gathered at the altar.

In the next chapter we will look at some of the "how-tos" for distributing the body and blood of Christ at Mass.

FOR YOUR REFLECTION

- The word Eucharist means thanksgiving. How does this understanding of the word affect your attitude toward your ministry?
- How do you participate in the eucharistic prayer? Do you have the sense that this prayer is prayed by the whole church or just the priest?
- In the early church, the entire eucharistic celebration was called the "breaking of the bread." What does this phrase signify to you?

FOR YOUR PRAYER

Reflect on the following words:

The cup of blessing that we bless, is it not a sharing in the blood of Christ? The bread that we break, is it not a sharing in the body of Christ? Because there is one bread, we who are many are one body, for we all partake of the one bread. (1 Corinthians 10:16–17)

DISTRIBUTION OF COMMUNION

The process for distribution of communion differs from parish to parish. Each parish needs to establish guidelines so that this process flows smoothly and reverently. Regardless of the procedure that is used, keep in mind that the eucharistic ministers—as well as all liturgical ministers—set an example for the assembly.

Receive, hold, and carry the vessels carefully and reverently. It should be common practice for ministers of communion to receive both the body and blood of Christ. *The General Instruction of the Roman Missal* states:

> Holy Communion has a more complete form as a sign when it is received under both kinds. For in this manner of reception a fuller light shines on the sign of the eucharistic banquet. Moreover there is a clearer expression of that

will by which the new and everlasting covenant is ratified in the blood of the Lord and of the relationship of the eucharistic banquet to the eschatological banquet in the Father's kingdom. (240)

It should not be the practice in any parish to go to the tabernacle for eucharistic bread consecrated at another liturgy. The Blessed Sacrament reserved in the tabernacle is for communion of the sick and for adoration. Everyone should receive from hosts consecrated at the liturgy that they have participated in, thus preserving the integrity of the celebration. The tabernacle should only be approached during Mass when a miscalculation has occurred and not enough consecrated bread was prepared.

According to the guidelines for your parish, ministers should move discreetly and purposefully but reverently to the locations from which they will distribute communion to the assembly. As you move to your assigned location, you should join in singing the communion song.

Ministers of the Bread

Once the ministers are in place distribution should begin. Allow yourself to enter into a faithful communion with those you are serving. If you are distributing the eucharistic bread, pick up one piece and hold it up to the line of sight between your eyes and the person to whom you are speaking. The eucharistic bread should not be raised above the two of you. If you are much taller than the recipient, you may need to bend to establish a sight line. On the other hand, if you are much shorter, you may need to look up to do the same. Personal presence to each communicant is of great significance. Ministers are an example of care and unity through their appreciation of and respect for those they serve. They help the assembly realize and establish communion with each other in the Lord Jesus.

One summer, my family and I hosted children from Belarus. These children had suffered the terrible effects of the Chernobyl nuclear disaster, and they had come to the United States for a time of respite and to renew their sense of hope. When they left our home to return to their country, we were heartbroken at the thought of never seeing them again. But on the Sunday following their departure, I experienced a powerful realization during the Eucharist that we meet each other every time we receive communion. We touch Christ as the body of Christ. And so indeed, we would again see our friends from Belarus in that regard.

As each person approaches you to receive communion, take time to look into the person's eyes and in a clear, gentle, audible but not loud voice say, "The body of Christ." This faith statement recognizes Christ in the breaking of the bread and it should never be modified, in any way, by the eucharistic minister.

It is also not recommended to use the person's name when they approach you to receive communion. This greeting is often intended to be inclusive, but the practice can be experienced in the opposite way because it excludes those whose names you do not know. Think about how you feel when you are away from home and you participate in liturgy as a stranger to the parish. If the minister is naming each person as he or she comes forward to receive, what happens when it is your turn? Do you feel a part of the communion or do you feel like an outsider?

After you clearly say "The body of Christ," wait for and listen for the communicant to say, "Amen." Note the body language of the communicant. Do they want to receive on the tongue or in the hand? If the communicant extends their hands, offer the eucharistic bread by placing it gently on the upraised hand with a very slight gesture of touch. If the communicant chooses to open their mouth and extend their tongue to receive, place the bread on the tongue without touching the tongue, if possible. (It is a very good idea to have a clean piece of tissue or a handkerchief within easy reach if you do touch the tongue. You may need to quickly but discreetly wipe your fingers before you give communion to the next person in procession.)

Sometimes, a person who is unaware of his or her surroundings will come forward in the communion procession to receive, such as an elderly person with Alzheimer's disease or a hurried teenager. I have found that by remaining truly reverent I am able to call them back to attention with a quiet word or gesture.

Look lovingly at each person as you minister the body and blood of Christ. You are a presence of Christ to each person as you minister, so smile tenderly and thoughtfully. Be aware of persons with disabilities. Eye contact is especially important with those who are hearing impaired, and touch is significant for those who are blind. A word of caution: this is not the time to correct people on the proper way to receive. I know of a eucharistic minister who could often be heard on Sunday morning throughout the communion procession scolding communicants for their unclean hands and poor posture. She would say things like, "Wash those hands," or "Stand up straight!"

If a piece of eucharistic bread drops to the floor, pick it up and either consume it, hold it discreetly in your hand under the plate, or place it to the side of the plate. It is important to remain calm at this moment and to reassure an anxious and embarrassed person that everything is all right.

Ministers of the Cup

By drinking from the cup we share in the Lord's cup of suffering. We express that we are ready to lay down our lives for another as Jesus did for us.

Before you begin distributing from the cup you should open up the purificator so that it can be used in multiple places during the distribution of the consecrated wine. The minister of the cup should hold the chalice before each communicant, look kindly into the communicant's eyes, and clearly state, "The blood of Christ." As mentioned before, this is a faith statement and should never by altered in anyway by the minister. The communicant will respond, "Amen."

Be aware that the person may not be planning to drink from the cup but has approached the cup in order to make a gesture of reverence to the cup, perhaps with a bow. This decision is the choice of the communicant. The minister should hand the cup to communicants, allowing them to take and drink from the cup. The communicant receives the cup from the minister, takes a sip, then hands the cup back. Use both hands to receive the cup back from the communicant. A small child or a person who is frail and weak may need you to hold your hands under the cup to catch it if necessary or assist the person in holding onto it. A blind person will need your guidance in accepting the cup from you and in giving it back to you. Again, be aware of people who are confused or inattentive. Take time to help each person receive according to his or her ability.

When ministering the precious blood, care must be taken to carefully wipe the rim of the cup inside and out using a new section of the purificator every time. If you need to change position of the purificator, do so. Then turn the cup approximately a quarter turn for the next person.

If you drop or spill the wine, immediately stop distributing from the cup. Quietly excuse yourself from your station. If the communicant caused the accident, take care to reassure him or her before leaving your station that everything is all right. Accidents happen! I once had a communicant's hand slip after receiving from the cup, and the wine spilled over the top of the cup onto the floor. I calmly placed my purificator over the spill and assured the woman that she had done nothing bad. Then I attended to the spill. Don't panic and draw attention to you or, more importantly, to the person involved in the accident.

If the spill is small, your purificator may cover it. If not, go directly to the sacristy for a large towel, cloth, or another purificator. Soak up the wine as well as you can, and then place a clean towel over the place. Resume distributing from the cup at a location away from the spill. Leave the spot covered until after Mass. After the liturgy, get a cold, wet cloth and carefully scrub the place where the spill happened. Any cloths used to clean up the spill should be placed with the purifcators to be rinsed out with the other sacred linens.

When there are no more communicants left to receive, follow your parish's guidelines for returning the unconsumed elements as quietly, efficiently, and reverently as possible. If you need to pass by the altar or tabernacle to return to the sacristy you should not make a gesture of reverence while carrying the consecrated elements. If you need to pass by the tabernacle or altar to return to your place in the assembly, however, you should always genuflect to the tabernacle and bow to the altar. Return to your place in the assembly and join in the communal silence or singing. The communion rite ends with the prayer after communion.

After the Mass has ended, eucharistic ministers may be expected to help clean and prepare the vessels for the next liturgy. In any case, do not rush out the door when Mass is done. Return to the entrance of the church and continue greeting and speaking with the community as they go forth.

Sending Forth

We are sent forth from the Sunday celebration of Eucharist back into our ordinary lives. Sharing in the Eucharist helps us to extend ourselves outside the liturgical context to our relationships in our daily lives. We are always in communion with each other. We carry the word of God out with us into our relationships. We are the living Christ in the world and we must bring the presence of Christ to others. The disciples on the road to Emmaus recognized Jesus in the breaking of the bread, then rushed back to town to share this discovery with their friends. We too must do the same.

In *Dies Domini*, John Paul II writes that our commitment cannot be restricted to the liturgical gestures of Sunday worship. He reminds us of how we are to continue our praise and worship of God by

> …inviting to a meal people who are alone, visiting the sick, providing for needy families, spending a few hours in voluntary work and acts of solidarity: These would certainly be ways of bringing into people's lives the love of Christ received at the Eucharistic table, not only the Sunday Eucharist but the whole of Sunday becomes a great school of charity, justice and peace.

We go forth in peace from the assembly with the gospel directive to love and serve the Lord. The work of God goes on.

FOR YOUR REFLECTION

- As a minister of the Eucharist, you treat people with reverence and dignity as they approach you in the communion procession. Do you do the same to the people you encounter in your everyday life? Remember, we are the body of Christ not just during liturgical celebrations, but always.

- What are some of the ways that you bring Christ to the world during the week?

FOR YOUR PRAYER

Reflect on the following words:

As you have sent me into the world, so I have sent them into the world. And for their sakes I sanctify myself, so that they also may be sanctified in truth. I ask not only on behalf of these, but also on behalf of those who will believe in me through their word, that they may all be one. As you, Father, are in me and I am in you, may they also be in us, so that the world may believe that you have sent me. (John 17:18–21)

BRINGING COMMUNION TO THE SICK

Because the sick are prevented from celebrating the eucharist with the rest of the community, the most important visits are those during which they receive holy communion. In receiving the body and blood of Christ, the sick are united sacramentally to the Lord and are reunited with the eucharistic community from which illness has separated them. (Pastoral Care of the Sick, 51)

Recently I was sick for several months and unable to be present for Sunday Eucharist. During the week many friends and parishioners took time to stop by my home with baked goods and meals for me and my family. But perhaps what meant the most of all was that each Sunday, someone brought me communion. This gesture truly helped heal and nourish me. I was physically missing from the assembly, but still sustained and supported by the community.

Oftentimes, eucharistic ministers who serve the parish community at Sunday Mass do not bring communion to the sick or the homebound. It is an important aspect of eucharistic ministry nonetheless, and a parish should have sufficient ministers trained and prepared for this work. The sick person is part of the body of Christ and their presence is missed during Sunday Eucharist. Eucharistic ministers who work with the sick and homebound bring the compassion and communion of the church to those unable to be present for liturgy.

> The faithful who are ill are deprived of their right and accustomed place in the eucharistic community. In bringing communion to them, the minister of communion represents Christ and manifests faith and charity on behalf of the whole community toward those who cannot be present at the eucharist. For the sick the reception of communion is not only a privilege but also a sign of support and concern shown by the Christian community for its members who are ill. (*Pastoral Care of the Sick*, 73)

Eucharistic ministers who are bringing communion to the sick are usually given the consecrated host after everyone has received communion and the communion vessels used at the altar have been cleaned. The blessed sacrament is carried in a pyx or small closed container. Those who carry the blessed sacrament are to protect it and never leave it unattended or let other activities distract them from their ministry.

The communion ministers may be publicly dismissed at the conclusion of the communion rite of Mass. Ministers should go directly from the Sunday liturgy to visit the sick person. They should be prepared to share a portion of the word of God with the sick person, as well as a brief reflection on the homily preached. They should never just drop off the blessed sacrament to a person's home or sickbed, but spend some time with them. The eucharistic minister may also wish to share the parish bulletin or news of the community during the visit. Remember, you are to bring compassion as well as communion.

The rite for the church's prayer when bringing communion to the sick and homebound is outlined in the book *Pastoral Care of the Sick: Rites of Anointing and Viaticum.* There are two principal forms of the Rite of Holy Communion to the Sick:

• communion in ordinary circumstances, which is used for a visit to a home or to a person in a hospital room and
• communion in a hospital or institution.

Both of these rites can be found in *Pastoral Care of the Sick.* Ministers should be familiar with the appropriate rite so that they are comfortable using it during the communion visit. They should be prepared to lead the prayers and know where to find the appropriate ritual and the accompanying Scripture. Every effort should be made to establish in each room at the bedside of each patient an atmosphere of faith and prayer. This time should not be hurried and the rite should never be diminished.

In addition to communion, you may want to bring a Bible for the Scripture readings, a white cloth for the table, a candle, holy water, matches, and a copy of the ritual for visiting with the sick. If possible, the minister should find out ahead of time if there are other family members, friends, or caregivers who will be present with the sick person who may also wish to receive communion. You may want to ask family members or caregivers to prepare a space for the communion service at the place where you will bring communion.

When you are visiting someone in a hospital or nursing home always make sure you check in with those responsible for the care of the person. The rules of the hospital or institution are to be strictly respected, and the eucharistic minister must be informed about procedural matters. Many facilities require frequent washing or scrubbing of hands and other protocols for contamination, and may require the minister to wear a hospital gown, mask, or gloves in certain circumstances.

At the end of the pastoral visit, the Eucharist is consumed, or returned immediately to the tabernacle of the church. Sick persons unable to swallow may receive communion under the form of wine. Our tradition does not reserve the Eucharist under this form. It must be brought directly from liturgy in a secure container and communicated with a straw, which can be used to place a few drops on the tongue, or a spoon, if the person is unable to drink. Consult the parish priests in advance on this matter.

The sick should have access to the sacrament of penance, as well. "The faithful are to look upon the eucharist as a remedy that frees them from their daily faults and preserves them from mortal sins" (*Pastoral Care of the Sick*, 11). You may learn of a desire for reconciliation from the person you are visiting, and you can then communicate this request to a parish priest.

Some years ago, I became ill and had to be admitted to the hospital. I found it interesting that when I was filling out all the necessary paperwork, the first question I was asked was whether or not I wanted a television in my room. The *second* question was whether or not I wanted someone to bring me communion. The next morning, I was astonished when a eucharistic minister stood in the doorway to my room and said, in a rather loud voice, "Would you like communion?" This was not at all what I expected in asking to receive the sacrament! Nevertheless, I responded "Yes," in a quiet, reverent voice. The minister then moved into the room, placed the pyx on the bedside table, opened the lid, and removed the host. Without hesitation she said "The body of Christ," to which I responded "Amen." She then said, "Have a nice day!" and off she went. Rather than feeling nourished, I felt very sad that this was the way I was offered the body of Christ, without ritual and prayers, just abruptly distributed. This situation would not have happened today with the effective training for eucharistic ministers that is available in most dioceses.

Like the disciples on the road to Emmaus we are on this journey together. We must share the good news with each other. As communion ministers to the sick, you are the living sign of the presence of Christ. You bring the gifts of compassion and comfort to those who are lonely, sick, in pain, or forgotten. Through this ministry of care, the sick are reminded that they too are part of the Body of Christ. They too are nourished and strengthened in the breaking of the bread.

FOR YOUR REFLECTION

- Think about a Sunday liturgy when you were unable to participate. What effect did your absence have on you? What effect might your absence have had on the rest of the community?
- Bringing communion to the sick and homebound is considered a ministry of care. In this ministry, how do you offer care and compassion to someone in need?

FOR YOUR PRAYER

Reflect on these words:

Blessed are the poor in spirit, for theirs is the kingdom of heaven. Blessed are those who mourn, for they will be comforted. Blessed are the meek, for they will inherit the earth. Blessed are those who hunger and thirst for righteousness, for they will be filled. Blessed are the merciful, for they will receive mercy. Blessed are the pure in heart, for they will see God. Blessed are the peacemakers, for they will be called children of God. Blessed are those who are persecuted for righteousness' sake, for theirs is the kingdom of heaven. Blessed are you when people revile you and persecute you and utter all kinds of evil against you falsely on my account; rejoice and be glad, for your reward is great in heaven, for in the same way they persecuted the prophets who were before you. (Matthew 5:3–12)

Resources for Further Reading

Author note: These resources have been helpful to me throughout my work in eucharistic ministry, as well as in the preparation of this book.

—. *Sourcebook for Sundays and Seasons.* Chicago: Liturgy Training Publications, 2001.

—. *The Liturgy Documents: A Parish Resource.* Chicago: Liturgy Training Publications, 1991.

Challancin, James. *The Assembly Celebrates: Gathering the Community for Worship.* Mahwah, NJ: Paulist Press, 1989.

Field, Rev. James A. *Full, Conscious, and Active Participation.* Washington, DC: Federation of Diocesan Liturgical Commissions (FDLC), 1997.

Finley, Mitch. *The Joy of Being a Eucharistic Minister.* New York: Resurrection Press, 1994.

Hughes, Kathleen. *A Mystagogy of Sacrament: Saying Amen.* Chicago: Liturgy Training Publications, 1999.

John Paul II. *Dies Domini.* An abridged version of this letter appeared in *Catholic Update*, March 1999 (Cincinnati, OH: St. Anthony Messenger Press).

Johnson, Lawrence J. *The Mystery of Faith.* Washington, DC: Federation of Diocesan Liturgical Commissions, 1999.

Kofler, Marilyn, SP and O'Connor, Kevin. *Handbook for Ministers of Care.* Chicago: Liturgy Training Publications, 1987.

Laverdiere, Eugene. *Dining in the Kingdom of God.* Chicago: Liturgy Training Publications, 1994.

Mahony, Cardinal Roger and the Priests of the Archdiocese of Los Angeles. *As I Have Done for You: A Pastoral Letter on Ministry.* Chicago: Liturgy Training Publications, 2000.

Philippart, David. *Saving Signs, Wondrous Words.* Chicago: Liturgy Training Publications, 1996.

Regan, G. Thomas. *The Sacristy Manual.* Chicago: Liturgy Training Publications, 1993.

Searle, Mark. *Liturgy Made Simple.* Collegeville, MN: The Liturgical Press, 1981.

Tufano, Victoria M. *Guide for Ministers of Communion.* Chicago: Liturgy Training Publications, 1999.

Worship Office, Archdiocese of Cincinnati. *We Gather in Christ: Our Identity as Assembly.* Chicago: Liturgy Training Publications, 1996.